Aliens Among Us: The Evidence

Extraterrestrial: Past, Present, and Future

Mari Bolte

Cherry Lake Press

Published in the United States of America by Cherry Lake Publishing Group
Ann Arbor, Michigan
www.cherrylakepublishing.com

Reading Adviser: Beth Walker Gambro, MS, Ed., Reading Consultant, Yorkville, IL

Photo Credits: page 1: ©MEDITERRANEAN/Getty Images; page 5: ©Alan Shepard/NASA.gov; page 6: ©JPL-Caltech/NASA.gov; page 9: ©ROGER HARRIS/SCIENCE PHOTO LIBRARY/Getty Images; page 11: ©D. McKay (NASA /JSC), K. Thomas-Keprta (Lockheed-Martin), R. Zare (Stanford)/NASA.gov; page 13: ©d-l-b/Getty Images; page 15: ©da-kuk/Getty Images; page 16: ©Cavan Images/Getty Images; page 19: ©NASA/NASA.gov; page 20: ©ESA/Hubble, M. Kornmesser/esahubble.org; page 21: ©NASA Ames/JPL-Caltech/T Pyle/NASA.gov; page 22: ©arianespace.com/NASA.gov; page 25: ©NASA/JPL-Caltech/NASA.gov; page 26: ©Yaorusheng/Getty Images; page 27: ©kali9/Getty Images; page 29: ©NASA/Paul Alers/NASA.gov; page 30: ©Spreadthesign/Shutterstock

Cherry Lake Press is an imprint of Cherry Lake Publishing Group.

Library of Congress Cataloging-in-Publication Data has been filed and is available at catalog.loc.gov.

Cherry Lake Publishing Group would like to acknowledge the work of the Partnership for 21st Century Learning, a Network of Battelle for Kids. Please visit *http://www.battelleforkids.org/networks/p21* for more information.

Printed in the United States of America

Mari Bolte has worked in publishing as a writer and editor for more than 15 years. She has written dozens of books about things such as science and craft projects, historical figures and events, and pop culture. She lives in Minnesota and loves looking up at the stars.

CONTENTS

CHAPTER 1

We're Not Alone

The next time you're outside at night, look up. Observe the stars. Are you curious about what life could exist out in space? Anything out there is probably just as curious to learn about you. Technology on Earth can't send the general public into outer space yet. But that doesn't mean advanced alien civilizations don't have the capability to reach outer space.

In 2020, an astronomer asked a question. He wondered if life would develop the same way if Earth got a do-over. Then he wondered what would happen if we had infinite numbers of do-overs. He concluded that there are four possibilities:

- Life is common and often develops intelligence.
- Life is rare and often develops intelligence.

Two dozen astronauts have traveled to the Moon. Twelve have walked on its surface. Pictured is Edgar Mitchell, who walked on the Moon on February 5, 1971.

THE GALACTIC FEDERATION

In 2020, Haim Eshed, a former space security chief from Israel, gave an interview. He said humans have been in contact with extraterrestrials. He said the aliens were part of a "galactic federation" and that they have an underground base on Mars. Officials from the White House, the Pentagon, and Israel stayed quiet. Eshed isn't the first high-ranking person to make this claim. Edgar Mitchell, the sixth person to walk on the Moon, said the U.S. government had proof of alien life too.

Exoplanets are also called extrasolar planets.

- Life is common and rarely develops intelligence.
- Life is rare and rarely develops intelligence.

Using what we already know about Earth, the odds that life is common was always nine times higher than the odds of life being rare. The odds of that life being intelligent was not as high. But there are an endless number of planets. Some estimate that there are 10 septillion of them. (That's a 1 with 25 zeroes after it!) The odds of none of those planets having any kind of intelligent life seem impossibly small.

The first living thing on Earth was microscopic. It showed up around 3.7 billion years ago. Modern humans have only been around for 200,000 years. Researchers believe

Mars could have hosted life 4 billion years ago. Martians had plenty of time to grow and **evolve**. Although scientists haven't found proof of life there yet, they haven't been looking that long.

And Mars isn't the only terrestrial planet that's like Earth. The first **exoplanet** to **orbit** a star similar to our Sun was discovered in 1995. Since then, more than 4,900 others have been found. The odds that our planet is completely unique are incredibly small. Learning about how life came to be on Earth—and how it might have been on Mars—can help us learn about alien life in the past, present, and future.

THE FIRST EXOPLANET

In 1995, astronomers Didier Queloz and Michel Mayor discovered the first exoplanet to orbit a Sunlike star. They called it 51 Pegasi b. It is 50 light-years away from Earth. The planet cannot support life. It is actually more similar to our Sun than our Earth. Scientists can't see exoplanets with a telescope. 51 Pegasi b was found because its gravity caused its star, which was visible, to wobble. When a wobble is spotted, scientists can assume there's a planet that's causing it. 51 Pegasi b is very close to its sun. It takes just 4 days to complete an orbit. It takes 365 days and 6 hours for Earth to orbit our Sun.

CHAPTER 2

Learning from the Past

What do we know about life on Earth? Learning how things survive here could hold the key to discovering evidence of life on other planets.

There are 8.7 million species of plants and animals on Earth. Some can fly. Others can breathe underwater. Some animals are highly intelligent and can solve complex problems. Others are fast, reaching speeds of 70 miles (113 kilometers) per hour. There are animals that can lift hundreds of times their body weight. There are enormous animals that can reach 100 feet (30.5 meters) long. Teeny tiny **organisms** called extremophiles can live in high heat, deep underground, at the bottom

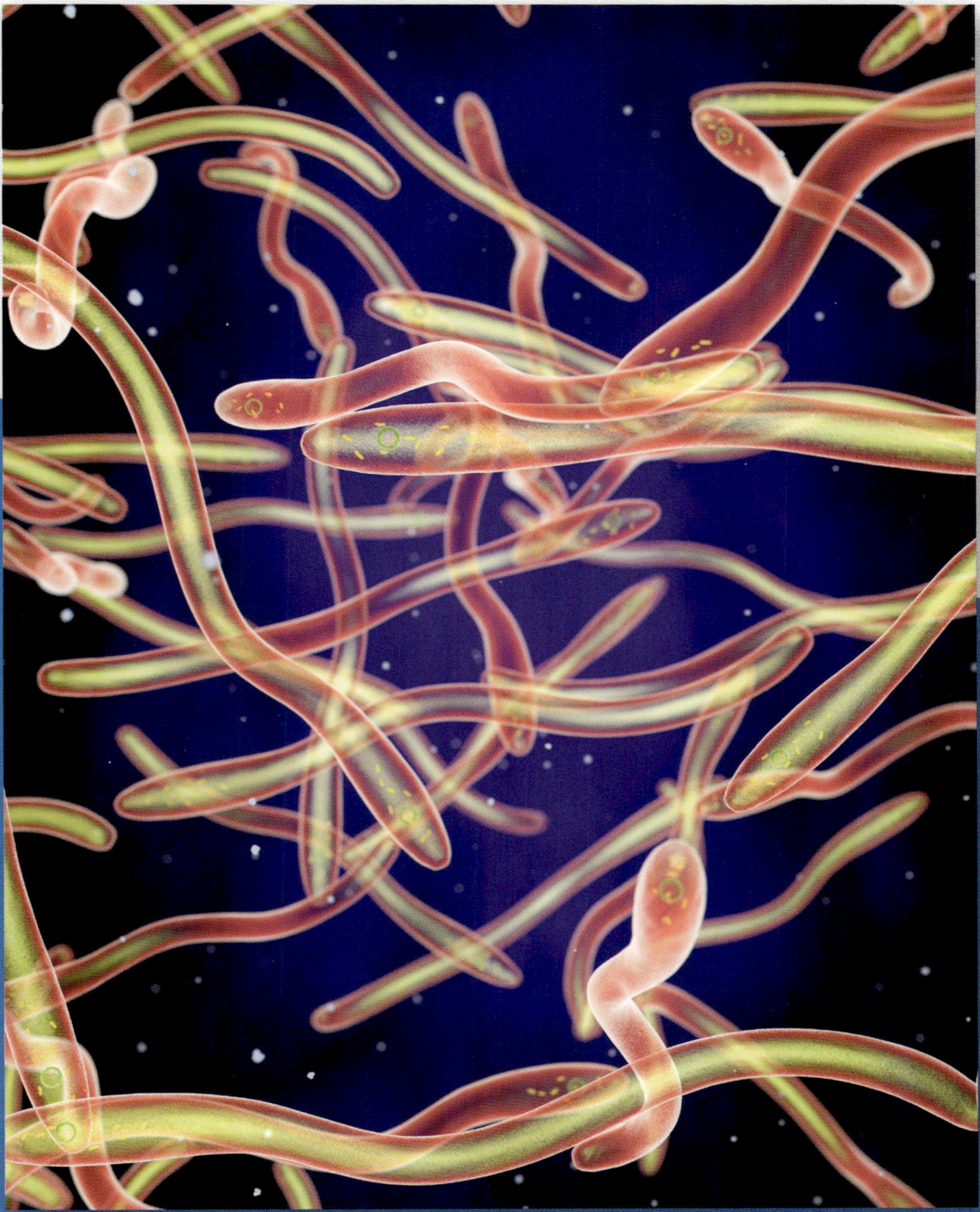

Some extremophiles can survive in multiple types of extreme environments at once. These bacteria live in hot springs.

of the sea, and inside of ice. Each animal has evolved to best fit its living situation.

In 2015, a biologist at Cambridge University spoke up. He said that humanlike extraterrestrials should have evolved on other Earthlike planets. Life on Earth developed in a predictable way. Life began and survived. More living things were born. They figured out the best way to live in their environment. They **adapted** over time. But there are only so many ways to grow an eye or an arm or a wing. Convergent evolution would guarantee that intelligent life that looks like humans—with limbs, heads, and bodies—could exist.

WHAT IS CONVERGENT EVOLUTION?

Convergent evolution is a process in which two distantly related things develop similar traits independently of each other. For example, sharks and dolphins are not closely related. They do not have a common ancestor. One is a fish, and one is a mammal. But they both live in the sea, so they need to be able to swim. They both developed long, slender bodies. They both have dorsal fins and flippers. Their gray color allows them to blend in when hunting. Their similarities exist because those traits are best for the animals' environments.

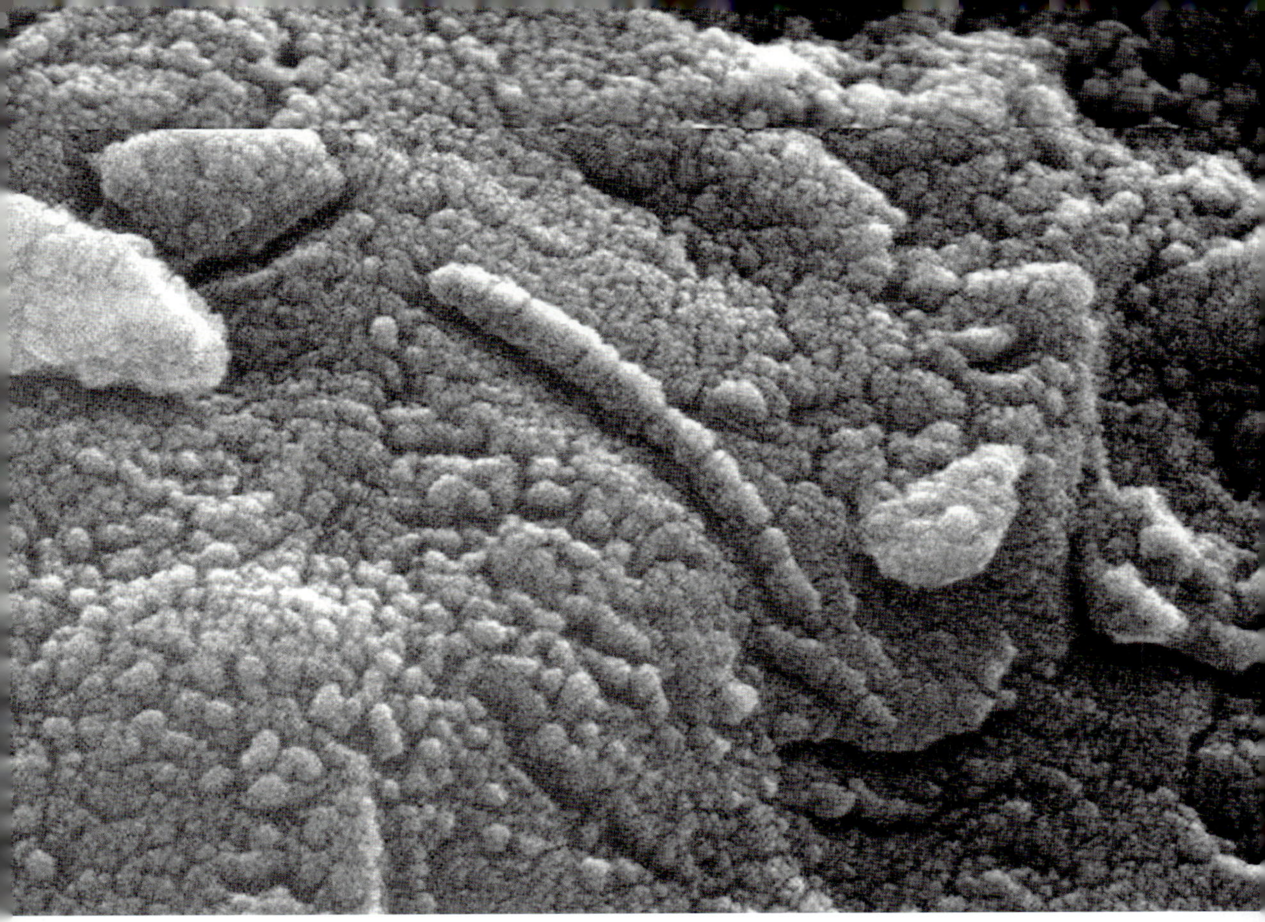

A meteorite with a fossil microbe was found in Antarctica. It fell to Earth 13,000 years ago.

Finding fully formed extraterrestrials would be an amazing discovery. For now, scientists are looking at the smallest living things—microbes. These tiny beings can only be seen with a microscope. Bacteria, fungi, molds, and viruses are all types of microbes. Scientists have also found fossilized microbes on **meteorites** that came from space.

In 1996, scientists from the National Aeronautics and Space Administration (NASA) announced they had found evidence of microbes on a meteorite from Mars. The meteorite had chipped off of Mars 16 million years ago when an asteroid or comet collided with the planet's surface. The meteorite orbited the Sun until about 13,000 years ago. Then it entered Earth's gravity and landed in Antarctica. The meteorite was more than 4 billion years old and likely existed when Mars had liquid water—and perhaps life. The scientists found crystals that could have been formed by ancient microbes. Interest from the findings led to today's exploration of Mars.

LIFE ON MARS

Since 1960, dozens of missions to Mars have taken place. Five space programs have landed on the planet. NASA's *Viking* **orbiters** and landers arrived in 1976 and sent information back to Earth for years. They looked for microbes but could not fully prove their existence. Launched in 1996, the Mars Global Surveyor arrived the following year. It helped future rovers land on Mars. Two of those rovers, *Spirit* and *Opportunity*, found evidence that water had once existed there. In 2019, *Curiosity* found evidence of methane, a gas that—on Earth—is created by biological life. The rover *Perseverance* began its search for life on Mars in 2021.

EVOLUTION

There is more than one way to evolve! Different animals evolve in different ways. Sometimes it results in similar features. At other times, it causes one species to branch into two or more species. Sometimes animals may die out—making room for new creatures to take their place.

Patterns of Evolution

Convergent Evolution

Different species gain similar traits. (Birds and bats both developed wings to fly.)

Divergent Evolution

Closely related species evolve to form a new species. (Zebras, donkeys, and horses all share a common ancestor but are different species today.)

Coevolution

Two or more species develop similar characteristics. (Cheetahs must be fast enough to catch gazelle; gazelle must be fast enough to escape cheetahs.)

Parallel Evolution

Different species develop similar characteristics even though they live in different geographical areas. (Tasmanian wolves in Australia and wolves in Europe developed skulls of nearly the same shape.)

Macroevolution

A large-scale change affects the entire species. (All whales evolved from a four-footed land mammal.)

Extinction

Evolution of new species causes the old species to die out. (About 250 million years ago, many large animals died out; their loss made room for dinosaurs.)

CHAPTER 3

Making a Connection

Finding microbes on Mars may be the next logical step to proving other life is out there. But microscopic creatures aren't as exciting as the idea of real, intelligent extraterrestrials! Ancient astronomers asked themselves, "Are we alone in the universe?" Astronomers today are still asking that question.

If intelligent life is out there, there would be telltale signs of its presence. Humans leave signs of being on Earth just by existing. These signs are called biosignatures. Oxygen is a biosignature. Plants and cyanobacteria produce oxygen as a by-product. Finding oxygen in another planet's atmosphere could lead to finding proof of life.

Light from cities on Earth can be seen from space.

LEAVING SIGNS

There are other ways besides radio signals to search for life. Physical proof could be one clue. Earth is surrounded by more than 27,000 large pieces of **debris**. This space junk is from artificial objects that were sent up there, such as satellites and pieces from spaceship launches. We have also sent things into space that won't be retrieved, such as rovers and orbiters. Aliens could find them. Or we could find theirs! Light pollution is another possibility. Light from cities on Earth can be seen from space. We might someday find another glowing planet in the universe.

Decaying plants create methane bubbles that form under icy lakes.

Methane is another gas-based biosignature. Methane is a greenhouse gas. Some of it is created in nature—cows and swamps release methane. But most of the methane on Earth is human-made. Landfills, burning fossil fuels, mining, and factories create huge amounts of methane. Searching for pollution in space could lead scientists to other advanced civilizations.

Technosignatures could be another clue. On Earth, we use **electromagnetic waves** called radio signals. A **transmitter** sends the waves through the air. A receiver picks up the waves. Then it turns them into sounds that can be heard through a radio. Aliens could know about this technology. Radio waves travel quickly through space. We could pick up on their signals. Then we could find out where they came from.

For more than 60 years, Earth broadcasts were sent over analog signals. These signals are sent as a continuous wave. Their strength and **frequency** can tell us what is sending them. They are high-frequency and high-power, so they are easy to pick up. Digital signals are sent as pulses at specific time intervals, not as waves. More information can be compressed and sent out. But the signals become weaker over longer distances. Since 2009, we have been moving toward digital transmissions. For example, cable TV is analog. But streaming services are digital. Aliens might not be able to find us if we've gone digital.

MISSED CALL

In March 2018, a student at Curtin University in Australia found a spinning unknown object in space. It released huge bursts of energy that had never been seen before. Three times an hour, it became the brightest source of radio waves visible from Earth. Then it disappeared. It was not very far away—about 4,000 light-years from us. That's about the same distance away as our nearest neighbor, the star Proxima Centauri. Some compared the object to a lighthouse in space. Was it a signal from an alien ship? Scientists are waiting to see if it shows itself again. They want to know more.

CHAPTER 4

Who Are You?

Earthlike planets are out there. The first exoplanet was discovered in 1995. Since then, more than 4,900 exoplanets have been found outside our solar system. Most of them were found thanks to the Kepler Space Telescope. There are thousands more that are still unconfirmed or undiscovered. The James Webb Space Telescope was launched in 2021. It will give us even more information about exoplanets and how the universe works.

Most exoplanets orbit stars the way Earth orbits the Sun. But other planets, called rogue planets, are out there floating alone. Some of the planets are rocky like Earth. Others are gas planets like Jupiter and Saturn. They all have **elements** that are found in our solar system. But they are all very different!

The Webb Telescope has 18 hexagon-shaped mirrors that are coated in gold. Gold is highly reflective. The mirrors are designed to collect light from objects far away.

K2-18 b was discovered in 2015. It is a rocky world that has both water and life-friendly temperatures. It is 124 light-years away.

Some planets are strange and unusual. Some are covered by oceans of water or fields of lava hot enough to melt metal. Some are shaped funny, thanks to the gravity of their stars. Others are near dead stars. They are cold and dark. Some planets might rain glass, or even gemstones! Somewhere out there is most likely an exoplanet that's like Earth. And one of those planets may be home to an advanced alien civilization.

Understanding life on Earth can help scientists understand what life on another planet might be like.

KEPLER SPACE TELESCOPE

Thanks to the Kepler Space Telescope, scientists believe there are more planets than stars in the sky. Kepler was launched in 2009. Its mission was to discover Earth-sized planets that orbited other stars in the **Milky Way**. It looked at stars and watched for planets that blocked the stars' lights as they orbited. Thousands of exoplanets were discovered. The telescope operated for 9 years. Its work will be continued with the James Webb Space Telescope.

The Webb Telescope was a $10-billion project that may answer some of our biggest questions about life in space. It was launched from an Ariane 5 rocket on Christmas Day, 2021.

But our human assumptions and **biases** might actually make it harder to search for life. One project, called Breakthrough Listen, is searching for signals of life. The project included **anthropologists** to help. Some scientists are part of the Search for Extraterrestrial Intelligence (SETI). Their goal is to find proof of extraterrestrial life. They might already have ideas about aliens based on what they know—or what they think they know. Anthropologists help them keep their ideas and expectations realistic.

Many SETI scientists believe we are looking for a version—or even a better version—of ourselves. But with that, we may assume that advanced aliens have our same sense of morals and ethics. We may hope that a message from space will tell us how to save our planet or solve a global problem like poverty. Anthropologists challenge that idea. Just because an alien species might be like us in some ways, it could be very, very different in other ways. They might not want to help us at all.

THE WEBB TELESCOPE

The James Webb Space Telescope was launched on December 25, 2021. It traveled 930,000 million miles (1.5 million km) and reached its final destination on January 24, 2022. It was the largest telescope ever sent into space. The Webb telescope uses **infrared light** to study the history of our universe. It takes time for light from objects in space to reach us here on Earth. For example, light from the Sun takes more than 8 minutes to travel to Earth. Some light we see has traveled for billions of light-years. Webb's infrared light will be able to "see" back in time. It should be able to see more than 13 billion years into the past, back when the first stars and galaxies were formed.

CHAPTER 5

Findings in the Future

Nothing will stop SETI scientists from their search for alien activity. Researchers from around the world have been watching, listening, and waiting since Frank Drake first pointed a radio antenna toward the sky in 1960. The SETI Institute was founded in 1984. Other SETI groups have been formed too.

Researchers need funding to continue their work. Governments and colleges are not always open to the idea of funding SETI research. In the 1980s and 1990s, NASA funded some studies to look for alien radio signals. But after government pushback, NASA was not allowed to fund SETI research after 1993.

The Goldstone Deep Space Communications Complex in California helps NASA connect to spacecraft exploring the solar system and beyond.

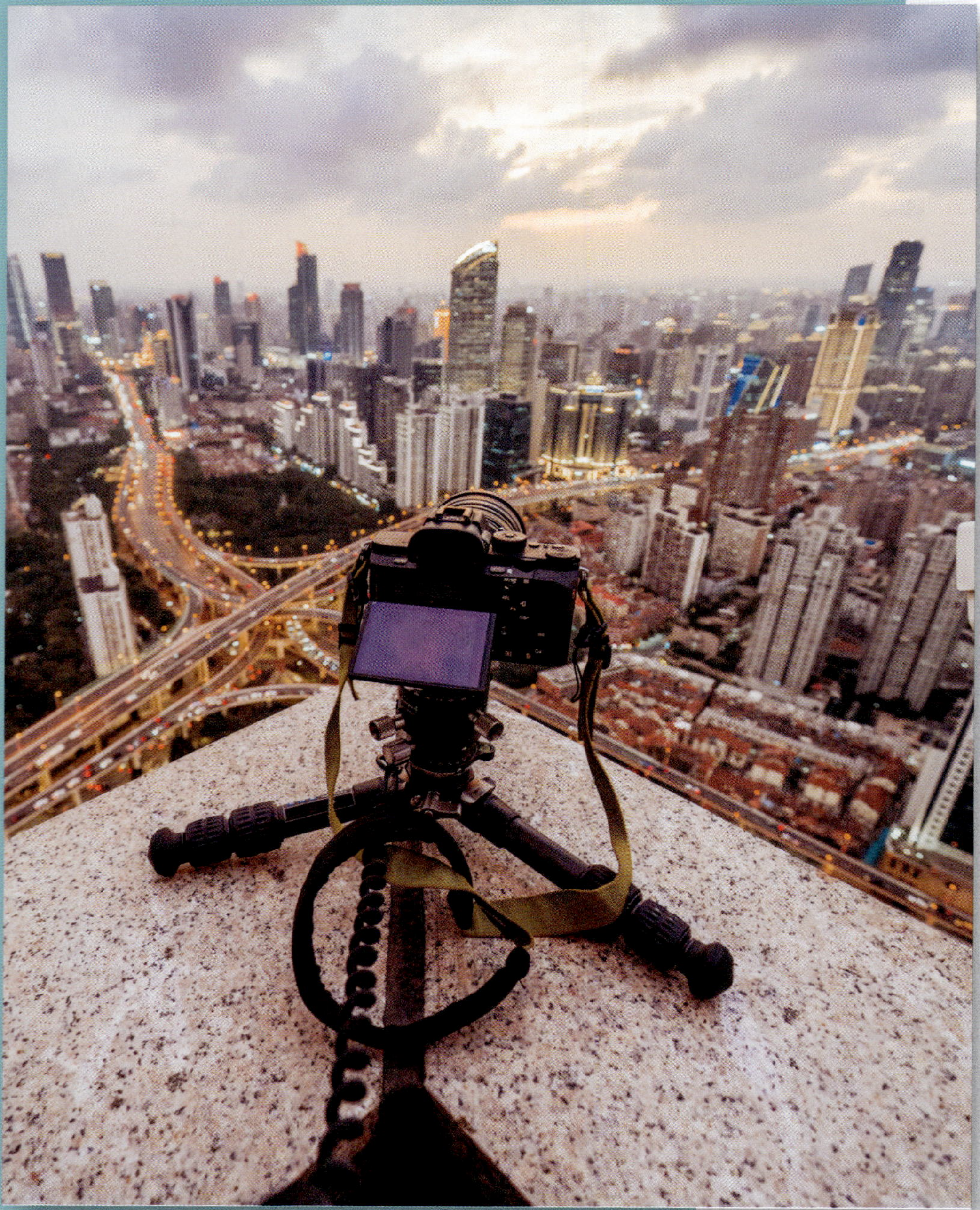

The Galileo Project wants to have more eyes on the sky in case unusual activity is detected.

Some researchers are turning to private sponsors. In 2021, Harvard astrophysicist Avi Loeb launched the Galileo Project with the sponsorship of a tech millionaire. The project uses rooftop cameras to hopefully spot any unidentified flying objects (UFOs) that enter Earth's atmosphere. Artificial intelligence will look at all the information and sort out anything that is not a UFO.

THE ZOO HYPOTHESIS

Some people believe that we haven't found aliens because they have already found us. They are making a choice not to contact us. Perhaps they are observing our species, as we do with animals in a zoo. Maybe they are quietly doing their own research. Maybe we're not as important as we think we are, and they're just ignoring our calls. Or maybe they're letting us live our lives in a natural way, without alien interference.

SETI@HOME

A program called SETI@home allowed everyday people to help with the extraterrestrial search. Participants downloaded a free program on their home computers. Each participant's computer, along with millions of others, would download and analyze radio telescope data. It was a way to distribute intensive work among many machines. It operated for 20 years, and more than 5.2 million people participated. The program was suspended in March 2020, when all the available data had finally been analyzed. But the website and message boards are still active for anyone interested. More volunteer work may be needed in the future.

The Breakthrough Initiatives were funded by billionaire Yuri Milner. Millions of dollars were granted to programs dedicated to answering the mystery of life in space. With that money, SETI scientists got access to some of the largest and best telescopes around the world. They received funding for engineering projects for missions into space. And scientists across disciplines were able to connect and discuss life in the universe.

Although physicist Stephen Hawking supported one of the Breakthrough Initiatives, he believed making contact with

Stephen Hawking believed that any aliens advanced enough to travel to Earth could be hostile.

aliens would be a bad idea. He believed we were not alone and wanted to find out if he was correct. However, he thought we should be cautious about answering back. Aliens might not see us as being as important as we like to think we are.

We will continue to wonder if we're alone until we find proof of life. Until then, we can learn from what we already know. We can ask questions, explore, and imagine. We won't know what else is out there until we actually make contact with other life-forms.

Activity

Alike, but Different

Think about some of the features humans have. We have heads, bodies, and limbs. We breathe oxygen. We use our eyes to see, our noses to smell, and our ears to hear. Choose a few human features. Think about why we have them, what they do, and how they help us live our lives. Then think about changes to our planet that might cause us to evolve differently. What if our air had less oxygen and it was harder to breathe? What if our planet was much hotter, or much colder? What if Earth's gravity was less, or more? Draw or explain these differences.

Learn More

Books

Finan, Catherine C. *Space Machines*. Minneapolis, MN: Bearport Publishing Company, 2022.

Morancy, Joalda. *Aliens: Join the Scientists Searching Space for Extraterrestrial Life*. New York, NY: Neon Squid, 2022.

Schaefer, Lola M. *Explore Telescopes*. Minneapolis, MN: Lerner Publications, 2023.

Troupe, Thomas Kingsley. *Searching for Aliens*. Mankato, MN: Black Rabbit Books, 2021.

On the Web

ESA: Life Around Other Stars
https://www.esa.int/kids/en/learn/Life_in_Space/Are_we_alone/Life_around_other_stars

National Geographic Kids: Mission to Earth
https://kids.nationalgeographic.com/space/article/mission-to-earth

The SETI Institute's Stuck at Home Survival Guide
https://www.seti.org/seti-institutes-stuck-home-survival-guide

What Is an Exoplanet?
https://spaceplace.nasa.gov/all-about-exoplanets/en

Glossary

adapted (uh-DAPT) became adjusted to new conditions

anthropologists (an-throh-PAH-luh-jists) scientists who study human behaviors and cultures in the past and present

biases (BY-uh-sehz) prejudices or beliefs for or against someone or something

debris (duh-BREE) scattered pieces of broken objects

electromagnetic waves (ee-LEHK-troh-mag-NEH-tik WAYVZ) waves of energy made by electric or magnetic processes that travel in a wavelike pattern

elements (EL-eh-mehntz) pure substances

evolve (ee-VAHLV) to develop gradually

exoplanet (EKS-oh-plan-eht) a planet that orbits a star outside the solar system

extraterrestrials (EK-struh-tuh-RES-tree-uhlz) beings from outside Earth

frequency (FREE-kwun-see) the rate at which something occurs or is repeated over a period of time

infrared light (IN-fruh-red LYT) electromagnetic radiation that cannot be seen by the human eye; we feel infrared as heat

meteorites (MEE-tee-uh-rytz) small rocky bodies from space that enter Earth's atmosphere and strike the ground

Milky Way (MIL-kee WAY) the galaxy that includes our solar system

orbit (OR-bit) the curved path of an object around a star, planet, or moon

orbiters (OR-bih-turz) spacecraft designed to orbit a planet

organisms (OR-guh-nih-zuhmz) individual animals, plants, or single-celled life-forms

transmitter (trans-MIH-tuhr) a set of equipment that can generate and send out electromagnetic waves carrying a message or signal

Index